BORROW TO GROW

Accessing Other's Achievements to Your Benefit

CHARLES MWEWA

DEDICATION

For

all those who are indebted to others,
in one form or the other.

CONTENTS

INTRODUCTION

The Power of Borrowing

Borrowing is an every-day routine among human beings. But borrowing is not just transactional, it is a necessity of life, and of success. The Dictionary defines to borrow as to "take and use (something that belongs to someone else) with the intention of returning it."

Thus, borrowing involves three factors: (1) Something that does not belong to you; (2) using it for something; and (3) with intent to return it to the original owner.

Due to inflationary and other economic considerations, we may add the fourth factor, (4) returning it to the original owner with some form of interest.

And finally, because simply borrowing may be imprisoning, we can encapsulate a fifth and last factor, (5) returning it with interest after securing the borrower's profitability. In summary, borrowing involves assets, diligence, contracting, interest, and profitability.

The contracting aspect of borrowing is implied, unless stated or modeled differently or otherwise. This means that when you borrow something, you must return it, with or without interest.

There are two types of borrowing, active and passive. In active borrowing, the lender and the borrower have a meeting of minds. They may agree to certain terms and conditions and may be legally bound to fulfil their part of the bargain.

Passive borrowing (which is the subject of this thesis) does not involve direct engagement between or among parties. It is enough to know that the borrower is using or taking another's assets, such as intellectual property or usages and utilities.

Thus, a borrower may not even be known to the lender, and vice-versa. The borrower must acknowledge in some form that what they took or used does not, or did not, belong to them but to someone else.

In this little treatise, we discuss four aspects of borrowing: Borrow to grow; borrow to know; borrow for tomorrow; and the four principles of borrowing.

1 | BORROW TO GROW

We borrow to grow, not to diminish. Whatever you borrow, you must grow. This is one of the ways in which borrowing is meaningful. There are four types of borrowing in the growing aspect. These are: Borrow other people's power; borrow other people's time; borrow other people's money; and borrow other people's achievements.

Borrow Other People's Power

If you have or lack power, you can borrow some. Powerful people can do what powerless people cannot do. They go where powerless people cannot. And they can get what powerless people cannot get. If you are powerless, you cannot move from where you are. You may be perpetually abused, be behind and stagnant. You must borrow from the powerful to move on to success. There are many ways of borrowing from the powerful, including:

- You can serve them.
- You can befriend them.
- You can join their ranks.
- You can follow them.
- You can advocate for them.
- You can give to their causes.
- You can endear them with gifts, praise or fluttery. And
- And you can marry into their families.

Once you become powerful, or associated with the powerful, you can do what the powerful can do. You can achieve the same success they can achieve.

Borrow Other People's Time

Time is limited. You cannot do everything you purpose to do in life within your life span.

You must improvise using other people's time. The people who achieved greatly even in the smallest space of time, such as Jesus Christ or Alexandra the Great, did the following:

- They invested in visioning; they shared their vision with those who would engineer it into action.
- They put time into human development, especially, of those who sympathized with their goals and dreams.
- They trained successors.
- They delegated authority and opportunities.
- They used other people's time; they listened and acted.
- They prioritized what they wanted to achieve before they died.
- They managed time carefully.
- And they minimized time wasting by multitasking.

Borrow Other People's Money

Borrowing other people's money is what most people do. They understand that they may not have all the resources to carry out their dreams, visions and plans. They may not have all the money. So, they borrow money. To successfully borrow and use other people's money, one must:

- Be honest.
- Repay it at the agreed upon time.
- Make effective use of the borrowed money.
- Factor in interest, if demanded.
- Be diligent.
- Diversify it, where necessary.
- Be responsible for gains and losses.
- And be ready to repay it on demand.

Borrow Other People's Achievements

If you want to achieve, you can only emulate and follow those who have already achieved. They are your short-cut to achievement. The principles that underlie achievement through borrowing may include:

- Study the achievements of others.
- Read autobiographies.
- Read and study biographies.

- Attend their meetings, if any.
- Invite them to presentations and seminars, etc.
- Use their techniques, with acknowledgment.
- Pattern one's work upon them.
- Go in the opposite direction to achieve the same results.
- And make them partners or friends, through mergers or ventures.

Conclusion

It is not necessary to rely only on your own ingenuity, money, achievements, time or power. These may be fickle.

It is important that you look to others and leverage their strengths to be your own. This is because life is both short and unpredictable.

This way, you may achieve more in a relatively shorter period of life on earth than if you overtly relied only on your own graces.

2 | BORROW TO KNOW

Borrow to know, not to compete. It is, usually, a major mistake when one wants to borrow another's techniques merely to compete. In life, knowledge breeds more explorations. It is better, therefore, to borrow to know than to compete. There are four types of borrowing to know. These are: Borrow other people's knowledge; borrow other people's wisdom; borrow other people's skills; and borrow other people's shrewdness.

Borrow Other People's Knowledge

Writers, researchers, and development workers borrow other people's knowledge all the time. In fact, there are nations which survive on borrowed knowledge. Indeed, there are movers and shakers who innovate knowledge and technologies, and others merely follow. But whether one individual or nation borrows from another depends on if they would acknowledge the primary source of the knowledge. In academia, failure to acknowledge the original source is known as plagiarism and may be ground for harsh academic penalties. In life, it is the same. The principles that underlie achievement through knowledge include:

- Borrow for a specific purpose.
- Do not plagiarize; acknowledge the original source.
- Aim to know more than what the original source knew.
- Use the acquired or borrowed knowledge to move far in life.
- When you know what another person or persons know, you can beat them at

their own game.
- Be humble and keep knowing more.
- And help those who do not know how to know.

Borrow Other People's Wisdom

Wisdom is not the same as knowledge, but it is related. Those who are wise must have knowledge or they know how to manipulate other people's knowledge for the good of all. Those who know may not be wise. The principles that underlie wisdom through borrowing include:

- Prudence. Wise people are cautious.
- Judgment. Wise people judge correctly; they are not biased, and they are fair.
- Thinking before talking.
- Paying attention to details.
- Reading many books; most of the time, the wisdom of the great is contained in books.
- Model through persuasive accumulation of knowledge of sages, gurus, religious movers, philosophers, and great thinkers.

- And applying wisdom to situations wisely.

Borrow Other People's Skills

It is common, in life, to borrow other people's skills. Although this is done through education, it can also be done by:

- Observation
- Apprenticeship
- Skills honing
- Volunteer work
- Part-time employment
- Reading books on specific topics
- Secondments
- Being mentored, etc.

Borrow Other People's Shrewdness

Call it smartness or frugality, or even geekiness, some people are just better at some things than others. You can borrow other people's shrewdness by:

- Paying attention

- Faithful service
- Convincing loyalty
- Being a consistent follower
- Asking questions and learning
- Not giving up on the quest to understand how the smart and their smart brains work.
- Giving heed to principles, formulae, and modeling.
- And thinking outside the box.

Conclusion

No matter how many books you may read on your own, you are limited to how much you can know and learn within your lifespan. It is vital, therefore, to leverage other people's insights, shrewdness, skills, wisdom, and knowledge to make headways in life. You can arrive at your desired destination easier by borrowing from others than by relying wholly on your own abilities, and mental and intellectual prowess.

3 | BORROW FOR TOMORROW

We may borrow not for today, but for tomorrow. Governments and families understand this approach. Some continents are wealthy today because of what their ancestors borrowed. They ensured that posterity would be served well. To borrow for tomorrow, you must do the following: Borrow other people's plans; borrow other people's experiences; borrow other people's examples; and borrow other people's models.

Borrow Other People's Plans

We may know the present, but we can only predict tomorrow. There are certain people who are skilled in the prediction of the future. We do not need to have their level of skillset, but we can borrow from them. To borrow other people's plans, we must:

- Understand or try to understand modeling (scientific or commonsensical).
- Invest time, energy, and opportunity in studying how the past generations defeated their challenges. This will help us to defeat the future.
- Have faith in the future.
- Not give up in the present.
- Not be discouraged by prevailing challenging circumstances.
- Not be limited by our education, background, or natural characteristics, such as tribe, color of skin, height, weight, national origin, etc.
- Review other people's plans and strategies.

- Use the plans that worked in the past.
- And gather the correct intelligence and information about our plans.

Borrow Other People's Experiences

The world is not linear, it is mostly spherical or round or cyclical. This is good news. It means that what you may be experiencing today, someone else has experienced it before. To borrow other people's experiences:

- Read many stories.
- Watch many moving pictures.
- Listen to the radio often.
- Read biographies.
- Read autobiographies.
- Listen to other people.
- Put yourself in the experiences of others.
- And know that history repeats itself.

Borrow Other People's Examples

While experience may be more related to instances, capabilities and encounters, examples are related to patterns, samples, and cases. To borrow other people's examples:

- Study models.
- Learn how others do or say or react in certain situations.
- Choose the right standards and follow them.
- Study cases and acclimatize your style and behavior to what works.
- Model your life upon what has worked for others.
- Believe in the *status quo* but go further and challenge it.
- And be a diligent follower.

Borrow Other People's Models

Models, experiences, experiments, and examples are related but they are not the same. The difference between experiences and examples were described in the previous section. Models go beyond and are more than just experiences and examples. They involve the following:

- Simulations

- Imitations
- Reproductions
- Replications
- Mockups
- Prototypes
- Templates
- Representations
- Samples
- Originals
- Illustrations

Conclusion

All these (plans, experiences, examples, and models) have one thing in common, they can yield identical or similar results in real life. Models simplify life and are key to quick success. By borrowing models, you can simplify your own journey to success.

4 | PRINCIPLES OF BORROWING

There are certain things that do not change. These are known as principles. They may be called thoughts, philosophies, doctrines, or moralities. They are universal in nature and are deterministic of the same results if applied correspondingly. We identify four principles of borrowing. These are: Borrow to return; return to multiply; multiply to benefit all; and benefit to profit.

Borrow to Return

A principle embedded in nature, and which must not be broken, is that when you borrow, you must return or payback. In nature, God lends us breath (life) and we must return praise. This applies in and to all things under the sun. This relationship may be termed symbiotic. When you borrow from someone, do not forget to return. Do everything to return what you borrowed. There are both natural and legal consequences of the failure to return. Avoid them.

Return to Multiply

Following the first principle, namely, borrow to return, it is imperative that the borrower makes the best use of the borrowed items, ideas, or ideals. To do so, the borrower must aim at multiplying the returns. In other words, the borrower must multiply what was borrowed to benefit others.

Doing nothing with what has been borrowed may subject the borrower to debt or prison.

It is the same in life, when one borrows ideas or principles, they must give credit to the original source. They must not hold themselves to be the origin of the ideas. In addition to that, they must make good on those ideas and please the original idealist. This is acceptable in nature, academia, and in business.

Multiply to Benefit All

Once borrowed, the borrower must aim to return and return with multiplied benefit. When God gives a talent, He expects His creatures to be responsible for it and to return it to Him one hundredfold. It is the same in nature.

When nature gives rain, it expects farmers to harvest more than they planted. One seed may be planted, but many grains are harvested. Borrowed items must be multiplied and benefit all. Everyone dies in life. The best form of living is the one that dies for others.

If you can distribute your efforts and energies to others, you might have lived a fulfilled life on earth. However, if you have been stingy and greedy, you would lose in the end. Someone who did not even work hard for it might inherit it.

That means that you may enter the afterlife with no credit to yourself. If you did use or distribute your wealth, inventions, and achievements as a service to and for others, you have a reward in the afterlife. Wisdom demands that you multiply your benefit to benefit all.

Benefit to Profit

The essence of life is profit. In each and everything God made, He put in it the potential for multiplication. That is profit. If you borrow another person's money, skills, models, examples, experiences, plans, shrewdness, wisdom, knowledge, achievements, time, or power, you must make profit out of them.

If you fail to make a profit, you will be stripped of what you initially received and left with nothing. In life, those who use ingenuity to manipulate resources are honored with more resources. They become or are deemed profitable.

If you fail to make profit from the borrowed money, you will end up indebted to the lender; that happens also with life. Therefore, when you borrow ideas or ideals, make profit out of them. That becomes sustainable success.

Conclusion

Borrowing is a good thing if you can return in time what you borrowed, multiply what you borrowed, benefit all with what you multiplied from borrowing, and make profit from what you borrowed and multiplied. Otherwise, it would be futile to borrow.

ABOUT THE AUTHOR

Award-Winning, Best-Selling Author, Charles Mwewa (LLB; BA Law; BA Ed; LLM), is a prolific researcher, poet, novelist, lawyer, law professor and Christian apologist and intercessor. Mwewa has written no less than 85 books and counting in every genre and has exhibited his works at prestigious expos like the Ottawa International Book Expo and is the winner of the Coppa Awards for his signature publication, *Zambia: Struggles of My People*.
Mwewa and his family live in the Canadian Capital City of Ottawa.

SELECTED BOOKS BY THIS AUTHOR

INDEX

Z